The Campi

by Paul Shipton

Illustrated by Alex Brychta

Say the sounds.

a e i o u s t p n m d g c

k –ck r h b f –ff l –ll –le –ss

j v w –x y z –zz qu

Blend the sounds to read the words.

family	supper	quick
stuff	hiss	struggle

The family went on a camping trip.
Dad had a plan for the weekend.

But the plan did not start well.
"We are lost!" said Mum.

It was getting dark when they got to the camp.
"We need to get the tent up quickly," said Dad.

They started to get the tent up.
It was a struggle as a bit of the tent
was missing.

Then they spotted a big bug in the tent.
"A beetle!" said Kipper.

They had to get rid of the beetle.
"This was not part of my plan," said Dad.

They went to unpack the rest of the
camping gear.
"We forgot a lot of stuff!" said Mum.

They had supper. Then Dad said, "We had better get to bed."
They got into the sleeping bags.

Dad said, "Can you hear that hiss?"
His air mattress had a puncture.

HISSSSSSs!

Soon the mattress went flat. It felt hard and bumpy under Dad.

In the morning, Dad was very sleepy.

"Have you got a plan for the next bit of the trip, Dad?" said Biff.

Dad had a quick look at his plan. Then it went in the bin.

"Just this," Dad said with a grin. "We will have lots of fun!"

Talk together

1. Why did the family arrive late at the campsite?

2. Why did Dad have a bad night's sleep?

3. Which of these objects are useful for camping?

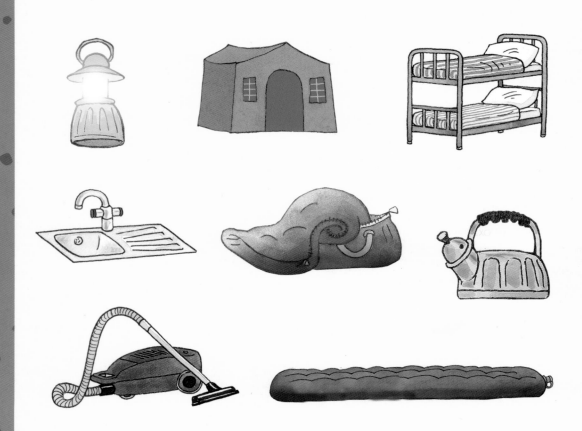